To:

_____

From:

_____

More
PRAYERS
ON
MY PILLOW

By Celia Straus

Prayers on My Pillow:
Inspiration for Girls on the Threshold of Change

More PRAYERS ON MY PILLOW

Words of Comfort and Hope
for Girls on the Journey to Self

CELIA STRAUS

BALLANTINE BOOKS • NEW YORK

A Ballantine Book
Published by The Ballantine Publishing Group
Copyright © 2000 by Celia Straus

www.randomhouse.com/BB/

Library of Congress Cataloging-in-Publication Data
Straus, Celia.
    More prayers on my pillow : words of comfort and hope for girls on the journey
to self / Celia Straus.
    p.   cm.
    ISBN 0-345-44195-8
    1. Teenage girls—Prayer-books and devotions—English.   I. Title.
BL625.9.T44 S76 2000
291.4'33'08352—dc21

                                                                        00-062118

Cover design by Min Choi
Cover illustration by Mirjam Selmi
Book design by H. Roberts Design

Manufactured in the United States of America

First Edition: November 2000

10 9 8 7 6 5 4 3 2 1

For my late grandmother, Geneal Condon, who gave me words of comfort and hope on my journey to self, who taught me to find gardens no matter where I was, and whose "still small voice" I hear every day.

Contents

Acknowledgments

First, my heartfelt thanks to Joanne Wyckoff, the ideal editor and my dear friend at Ballantine, who provided immeasurable support for this book and the previous one, championing both through the past three years with commitment, enthusiasm, creativity, and intelligence. A special thanks to my agent, Sarah Jane Freymann, whose grace under fire is an inspiration to me; to Allison McMillan Lee, who, like my daughters, understands the importance of having a new prayer every day; to Janet Fletcher, whose perception, clarity, and empathy as a copy editor is unrivaled; and to Susan Piver Browne, my producer and soul mate, who "hears" the prayers as I do, spoken from the heart and surrounded by music.

In memory of a loving champion and mentor, Holt Riddleberger.

My gratitude also to Karen Allyne; Denise Baddour; Carolyn Bain; Josh Baran; Ruth Bollinger; Father Harold Bradley; Ruth Blount; my dear parents, Ray and Patricia Brim; my aunt, Katherine

Brim; Cherie Burns; Linda and Michael Chambers; Rich Devane; Shireen Dodson; Father Gregory Eck; Julie Collins; Dr. Carolyn Erickson; Louise Garlock, my high school "best friend"; Elinor Hall; Judith Ivey; Catherine Lee; Dr. Rick Levy; Reverend James Lisante; Toby Marquez; Cindy Martin; Reverend Sandra Mayo, whose wisdom continues to sustain and guide me; Robin Olson; Maggie Petito; Mary Preston, who sends me lions; Dennis Reeder; John Romano Jr.; Alison Silver; Paula Silver; Jennifer Stockman; Charyn D. Sutton; Dr. Raymond Tanter and Constance Andersen Tanter; Dr. Jeanine Turner; Dr. Robert Thomas; Nancy Van Gulick; Armstrong Williams; Angela Stent; and Daniel Yergen.

I am deeply indebted to many writers and teachers whose works have challenged and inspired me since I started this project. These works include Frederic and Mary Ann Brussat's *Spiritual Literacy*, Julia Cameron's *The Artist's Way*, Laura Cerwinske's *Writing as a Healing Art*, Thomas Dubay's *Fire Within: St. Teresa of Avila, St. John of the Cross, and the Gospel—on Prayer*, Anne Lamott's *Traveling Mercies: Some Thoughts on Faith*, Robert M. May's *Physicians of the Soul: The Psychologies of the World's Great Spiritual Leaders*, Kathleen Norris's *Amazing Grace: A Vocabulary of Faith*, and just about anything by Frank Channing Haddock, C. S. Lewis, Thomas Moore, Florence Scovel Shinn, or Chogyam Trungpa.

Finally, there is *Upholding Mystery: An Anthology of Contemporary Christian Poetry*, edited by David Impastato.

I've also been blessed with an incredibly supportive family. My daughters, Julia and Emily, have been troopers. Although I still write prayers for them upon occasion, we all agree that what happened during two years of intimate correspondence was the beginning of something much greater than simply a mother/daughter dynamic. And it is that small miracle which continues in this book. Finally, my husband, Richard, has been something of an unsung hero. He has been totally supportive of a book and a calling that focused on girls in general and his wife and daughters in particular. Often people ask if I am married and do not wait to hear the answer. Richard likes to joke that perhaps he served his purpose some dozen years ago. But more important than any practical advice he may offer, it is his love and understanding of my prayers that help me to carry on. You see, fathers were once teenagers, too.

We're All More Than What We Seem

This book is a sequel to *Prayers on My Pillow: Inspiration for Girls on the Threshold of Change*, a collection of 150 prayer-poems selected from the hundreds I wrote for my daughters—Julia, then twelve, and her younger sister, Emily, who was eight. Beginning in October 1995 and continuing for almost two years, I wrote a prayer-poem every night. I began writing the prayer-poems because Julia was distancing herself from me. The project was my effort to bridge the gulf that was developing between us as she confronted the confusion, the changes, and the pressures of growing up, and I confronted the accelerated pace of life that leaves many of us parents with little time for heartfelt conversations with our children. I wrote them because both of us needed a way to handle this time in our lives with grace and courage and love. The prayers were *indirect* expressions that let her know I understood how she was feeling and what she was going through, and they were attempts at finding points of entry into her interior life, which was closed to me. A few months into the project Emily noticed the prayers being left on Julia's pillow and asked that I write ones "just for her," which I did. They didn't solve all my daughters' problems, but they did keep the connections between us intact.

When the book came out in the fall of 1998, neither I nor my two daughters had any idea how it would be received. However, the overwhelmingly positive responses shouldn't have surprised us. What is most real and personal in our lives is also what is most universal in the lives of others. Our inner selves yearn for truth and for the recognition of Spirit. Any expression of the interior journey of adolescence, in concrete and credible terms that ring true, meets this urgent yearning at its most basic level. The form of expression I choose, prayer-poetry, recognizes and respects the interior life of an adolescent girl—or, as I discovered from moms who have become avid readers of the prayers as well, anyone who has ever *been* an adolescent girl. In fact, the inspiration for this second volume comes from the reactions of so many girls and women to the first book. Most of these prayers I wrote in response to requests for prayers that came to my Web site, www.girlprayers.com.

I first established the Web site to support the book. But I soon discovered that girlprayers.com had become a kind of on-line youth ministry, providing support and solace for girls and their families as they weathered the stormy times that inevitably occur in any and all relationships. Some months nearly a hundred thousand people visit the site, and each day I receive dozens of personal requests for individualized prayers. I hear from teenage girls who are hoping to find, through spirituality, the answers to problems such as peer pressure, eating disorders, loneliness, depression, parents' divorce, substance abuse, and, of course, boys and sex. I also hear from those teenage girls' mothers, sisters, relatives, and friends who are seeking to stay connected as the girls go through adolescent changes.

This collection of prayer-poems, like the original one, is written in the first person. The prayers address life's rhythm of successes and failures with words of compassion and courage that invite personalization and ownership on the part of the reader or, better yet, the *listener*. The more prayers I write, the more I realize that prayer is far more about *listening* than speaking, that we all are like the Hebrew prophet Elijah, who heard the Lord, not in the storm, neither in the earthquake nor the fire, but in that "still small voice." My "still small voice" speaks in poetic forms that center on using the journey to self-knowledge to cope with life's problems, to live life more fully, and, in the process, to discover the Divine within.

Many of us forget who we are as we grow up. We no longer hear that inner voice that was so clear and joyous when we were children. Often the forgetting starts to happen when we are around ten or eleven. During the past two and a half years of reading thousands of e-mails and speaking to numerous groups of parents and teens, I have found that young people yearn to hear that voice as clearly as they once did. Their search for self and for faith in a Divinity greater than themselves is, I believe, an attempt to gain a sense of life's purpose. I hope these prayer-poems facilitate their search and provide a path toward wholeness and balance.

If a math teacher wanted to create a formula illustrating how these prayers help girls achieve balance, she could express it like this: CI (correct interpretation) + RA (right adjustment) = B (balance). For teenagers, it's a significant revelation to learn that, in the midst of all their confusion and searching, they have it within their power to correctly interpret an event and their feelings about it, and then adjust their response in a way that allows them to cope *and* grow stronger. When the power of self is moved from some abstract concept on the edge of a young person's life into her very core, a girl finds new ways of thinking about herself and her relationships with others. This approach to spirituality breaks down barriers, builds bridges, and relaxes the often rigid and harsh standards by which teenage girls judge themselves and their peers.

The balance achieved through any single prayer may be ephemeral, yet even a *temporary* feeling of connectedness and well-being strengthens and clarifies belief and understanding of oneself. Given the disintegration of family structures and the frantic pace of modern life, it is difficult if not impossible to find time to examine what is real versus what is imagined. I have ceased to be surprised at how often the issue of time crops up in the e-mails I receive: "no time to study, so I'm stressing out over grades," "no time to talk to my mother [or daughter] and she is driving me crazy," and so, needless to say, "no time to figure out how to talk to God." The Internet itself, the very medium through which girls communicate with me, intensifies this time pressure. No one writes letters or even complete sentences any longer—not when they can send an instant message packed with shorthand expressions.

So I think of these prayer-poems as small gifts of *time*, whether e-mailed or read from a book. They are usually opened at the end of the day, offering an opportunity, however brief, for solitude to reflect and find comfort. They are problem-specific Acts of Faith that work wonders simply because each prayer replaces negative energy with positive. As their creator, I am particularly grateful for the time it takes me to focus my attention inward to *listen*, and often, as I reflect on what to write, to recall and feel the emotions and confusions about identity that *I* experienced as an adolescent.

I grew up an "Air Force brat," and during my middle school years, from sixth to tenth grade, life seemed unbearable. I was changing schools at least once each year. Each move to a new air base meant adjusting to a new environment and making new friends. I remember myself at age eleven, standing fearfully outside a seventh-grade English class at the base school on the outskirts of Tokyo trying to get up the nerve to open the door. I was tall for my age, gangly, with braces on my teeth, thick eyeglasses, and more than a few pimples. I had absolutely no self-confidence and not a clue about how to act in order to be accepted and liked.

So I started reinventing myself. By eighth grade, at another school, I was "Sam," the tough girl, an early sixties version of Rizzo in *Grease*. I wore a leather jacket and used to sneak out of the house to ride around Tachikawa Air Base on the back of my boyfriend's motorcycle. I was constantly in trouble with my parents, "grounded"—in today's vernacular—on a regular basis. I was angry, fearful, guilt-ridden, and most of all confused about who I was. In ninth grade I attended Bellingrath Junior High in Montgomery, Alabama, as "Toni," from France, complete with French accent. I'm unsure why I thought I could maintain this identity without actually *speaking* any French, but I managed to charm both peers and teachers for weeks before being found out. My public humiliation and my shame were worse than any punishment my parents could have meted out. Practically every day I receive e-mails from girls experiencing these same feelings—under different circumstances. In an instant I am transported to my past, so as I write prayer-poems for them, I too can experience the joy of finding out who one really is and then having the courage and honesty to be that person.

As someone whose credentials in prayer writing are only those of a mother who deeply loves her daughters, I have only my own experience and ability to offer here. For me, prayer is both intimate and specific. This is why, as with the first book, I have organized the prayers by topics that girls confront every day—from peer pressure, isolation, and fear to celebrating a victory, making a decision, and giving back to your community. When we use poetry as the vehicle for expression, the message we wish to communicate circumvents our left brain, the part that judges, censors, rationalizes, and plans. We connect instantly and directly to our inner selves.

Once, when I was speaking to a large group of parents, someone commented that all the prayer-poems I write are childlike and simplistic in terms of rhyming and vocabulary. I answered that the voice of the inner self *is* a child, and we can reach teens better if we adopt that voice. I also think that the longings of the human soul are the same regardless of our religious persuasions, and that prayer does more than enable us to look deep inside for courage and comfort. Prayer enables us to triumph through love by having a relationship with something greater than ourselves—with Divinity—with God.

COURAGE
FROM
WITHIN

I think I'm afraid to grow up, God,
For I see how much pain there can be.
I want to stay young and protected.
I'm scared that I'll lose what is me.

I think I have courage to trust, God,
That I'll do just fine with what's new,
For Love stays inside me forever.
As I grow, my faith grows in You.

No matter where this life takes us,
Together we shall persevere.
Each test builds courage, makes us stronger—
A family based on faith, not on fear.

This family is calm when around us
People argue, cry, and fight.
This family is clear when around us
Others cannot find the light.

We find joy when all around us
People cry in their despair.
We know Love when all around us
Others seek but know not where.

I am not alone
As I walk hunched down hallways
Or hold my lunch tray looking
For a friend and finding only
An empty seat at an unfriendly table . . .
As I enter a classroom late and nervous
With all eyes judging
Or dress after gym without showering
To avoid being watched . . .
As I stand outside the circle,
The gang, the group, the crowd,
Living my life in isolation
Pretending I don't care.
Let me remember *I am not alone*.
God is with me—His angels surround
And deep inside are the loving
Voices of generations of souls like me.
I am not alone.

When people tell me I must change
To win their friendship, help, or love
May I have courage to say to them
I change each day, transforming to
A better self, but not for you.

When people tell me I am wrong
Because I don't do what they want
May I have courage to say to them
These things I do are from the heart—
Nothing you say can change that part.

May I have the courage to start over again,
May I reach deep down to my core
And find what it takes
To play for high stakes
Because that's what I'm aiming for.

May I have the strength to face down loss,
May I push past all of my fears
To aim for the heart,
Where I'll touch the part
Of the self who can smile through my tears.

May I have the trust to get past the test,
May I find in my failures the key
To unlock the door
That opens to more
Than I ever believed I could be.

Let me stand proud, straight, and tall.
Let my courage empower me.
Let me live each day with laughter.
Let my gifts shine for all to see.

Keep me strong when I am tempted.
Keep my tears for those I trust.
Keep me calm amid confusion.
Keep me safe from dawn 'til dusk.

I must not feel guilty—
I'm neither bad nor wrong.
No matter what the others think,
I know where I belong.

I must not feel guilty—
My path is straight and true.
And even though I'm criticized,
I believe in what I do.

I must not feel guilty—
For God is One with me.
God's Love lights up my heart and soul.
From guilt, I am set free.

I pray to be free
Of my demons within,
Their voices demanding
I keep very thin.

I pray for the strength
To ignore what they say
When they tell me to starve myself
All through the day.

I pray I can praise
What I see in the mirror—
A body that's nourished
With love, not with fear.

May I be strong-willed and calm
When turmoil whips me around.
May I be firm and yet kind
With those who try changing my mind.

May I be steadfast and brave
When others refuse to behave.
May I be joyful and free
With the beauty life offers to me.

May I be patient and true
When I feel like I haven't a clue.
May I be faithful and clear—
With my strength, there is nothing to fear.

Help me find courage deciding
When decisions aren't easy to make
When choices can go either way
When results won't be easy to take.

Show me my strength in the seeking
When solutions aren't easy to find
When only my self offers answers
To decisions essentially mine.

BREAKING
DOWN
MY WALLS

Let me delight in the beauty
Of this glorious world that I see.
Let me be calmed by the sunlight
That pours golden warmth down on me.
Let me take joy in the breezes
That blow off the ocean so near.
Let me breathe deep and be open
To a world where there's nothing to fear.

Behind all their wrinkles and age spots
Is the heart of a child much like me.
So let me not judge the old folks,
They offer far more than I see.

When I get impatient with their stories,
Dismissive of all that they say,
May I listen to what they can teach me,
Grow connections between us that stay.

May I reach out to someone who needs me
    Someone who's lonely
    Someone who's shy
    Someone who's quiet when others are talking
    Someone whose smile
    Is hiding a cry.

May I make friends with someone who needs me
    Someone who's left out
    Someone who's new
    Someone who's searching for a place to fit in
    Someone who's wanting
    Someone like me, too.

Why is it so difficult to trust them?
Why is it impossible to care?
Why, when warmth is offered, am I frozen?
Why, when they reach out, am I not there?

Why, though every day I wake up lonely,
And waking, search for love I cannot find,
Am I unable to return their smiles—
So afraid they'll see into my mind?

Why have I built walls I will not scale
When I so desperately want to get out?
My world is locked. I've lost the combination.
I'm safe inside, but what else have I got?

Please, help me open up my heart
To all that life is meant to be.
I'll start with just the simplest gesture.
I'll offer the Love that's part of me.

When I sing my songs
Or write my poems,
A part of my self is revealed
A part of my heartache is healed.

When I play my notes
Or dance my steps,
A part of my feeling is known
A part of my talent is shown.

When I draw my scenes
Or sculpt with clay,
A part of my dream is released
A part of my soul is at peace.

I keep myself closed to people around me,
Often just smile and utter no sounds.
If there is a way for me to survive,
Then please talk with me so I feel alive.

I keep myself separate, alone and away
From those who look past me, day after day.
If there is a way for me to go on,
Then please touch my heart so I can be strong.

What does it take to be happy?
Where do I look to find hope?
What does it take to have peace?
How in my life shall I cope?
What does it take to feel love?
When does my heart open wide?
What does it take to touch joy?
When I look and find You, God, inside.

When I stand in front of others
To show what I can do,
May whatever I am offering them
Be a part of me that's true.

Let me feel my power from deep inside
And once I start to play,
May I lose myself in what I'm doing
And be joyful this day.

My words come from my inner self,
My notes come from my heart,
And all the work and practice
Reveals my artist's part.

The same holds true for all of life—
Each day can be a test
Of how I stand, my head held high,
To do what I do best.

Have I hidden myself behind labels?
My name, race, generation, or grade?
I'm caught in a web of conventions
Which I've allowed to entangle me.

Let me escape this trap of closed thinking,
Let me be more than what others create.
For what I am really defies definition—
My soul is the essence of me.

*M*ay I find a way to bring out the best
In the people I meet each day:
To look clearly
At what makes them special,
To listen carefully
For words that welcome me in,
To speak gently
Of things that bring us closer,
To experience honestly
The feelings between us,
To focus
On building a bridge between us.

SLEEPLESS NIGHTS

When no one understands me,
When no one wants to hear,
When no one thinks I should be sad
Or be in pain or fear,

When no one sympathizes,
When no one cares a lot,
About the worries inside my heart,
About the things I'm not,

When no one has ten minutes' time,
When no one can advise,
Or help me clarify my life,
When my whole life is lies,

Then out of desperation
I look inside and pray.
I trust that You are listening
To all I need to say.

Please help me find my self.
I woke up lost again
My mind a blank
A stranger where
There once had been a friend.

I do not know what words to say
Or how I should respond.
I'm paralyzed,
Insensate, for
My self has come and gone.

My choices overwhelm me
When there's no path to take.
It's chaos here
Confusion reigns
My feelings all are fake.

I'm starting out so empty
Alarmed I'll be found out
I'm so alone
Surrounded by
Strong selves who have no doubt.

Please help me find a touchstone
A glimpse of self to see
That I can follow
Through the day
Until I locate me.

Help me, God,
I'm so confused
I'm so mixed up
I wish that life
Would slow and stop.
Too many choices
Too much to do
I'm tugged and torn
This way and that.
I can't see clear
What's best for me
And so I worry
And pace the floor
My hands clenched tight
My stomach tense
Afraid that You
Will let me fall
Because I cannot
Do it all.

I pray that tonight will work out.
I believe that tonight I will see
A new way to act
Instead of the trap
That often imprisons me.

I pray that tonight will bring news.
I trust that the headlines will state,
She's started to change
Begun to arrange
A new life before it's too late.

I pray that tonight will allow me
To do what I know I must do
I will stand my full height
And choose what is right
To be honest, courageous, and true.

When my voices keep talking, my worries keep
    knocking,
And I toss and I turn through the night,
When my guilt overcomes me, my fears overrun me,
Yet I dare not turn on the light,

When I'm begging for comfort, obsessed with some
    hurt,
And I whisper pleas to the air,
When my poor mind is racing, my demons are
    chasing,
Yet the comfort I seek isn't there,

Then let me stop stressing, instead find a blessing
In the peace and the calm of belief
That You really love me and could never be angry
And sweet dreams will be my relief.

I sit by myself
Alone at night
Through tears of frustration
I talk to God.

Sometimes I'm thankful
More often I question
Trying to find answers
I talk to God.

Asking forgiveness
For daily offenses
Feeling so guilty
I talk to God.

Stumbling words
Expressions of anguish
Searching for comfort
I talk to God.

Let me sleep the night away
Let my mind be still
Let my body's tension leave
Let my memory fill
With one moment of pure bliss
To calm my waiting soul
With hope the same will come tomorrow
As I play out my role.

Let me sleep the night away
Let my voices cease
Let my eyelids gently close
Let my worries release
For I have done my best today
There's no more I can do
Except to thank You for Your love
That keeps me close to You.

Let me sleep
Let my mind calm
Let my heart be full of peace
Let my worries flee
Let memory of one joyful moment soothe
The hurts and the pain of today
Let my body be still
Let me sleep.

Why do I feel so sure I've done wrong,
So fearful my world's about to collapse?
What inside me is so insecure
That I look over my shoulder and under my bed
Searching for monsters just like before,
Striving to please, to be perfect and pleasant,
Because if I'm not, and the truth is found out
That the monsters are me, then what will happen?

You will love me . . .
and nothing will happen but love.

I wish this day were not over
It all went by far, far too fast.
I grabbed at each moment of pleasure
Hoping to make the hours last.

I know I should simply be thankful
For all that has happened to me
But I can't help being sorry it ended
For my achievements were glorious to see.

Yet the bliss of one day is so fleeting
Dark night falls and joy fades away.
So let me put all today's memories
In the place where I go when I pray.

OVERCOMING
MY FEARS

When I'm so surrounded by life's demands
I wake up in a tomb
When every moment is a trap
And every word a wound

When I can't listen to my songs
For fear I'll come undone
When my heart is frozen, hard as ice
And my soul has cut and run

Please let me find just one small crack
In this eternal night
And open wide this house of fear
To let in Love's pure light.

I'm so afraid. I don't see how
I'm going to make it through this day.
I need faith in You
Or I will break.

I'm so unhappy. I can't find one
Single part of my life that's turning out.
I need joy in You
Or I will break.

I'm so guilt-ridden. I hate the
Things about myself that I know are weak.
I need strength in You
Or I will break.

I'm so confused. I don't know
Where to turn for help. There's no one there.
I need to trust in You
Or I will break.

When fear is what I feel
So helpless
So unsure
My stomach in knots
My heart beating fast
And instinct tells me to run away—
Let me stop instead and pray.

When fear is what I feel
So paralyzed
Such pain
My muscles tense
My voice shaking
And my mind cries out in fright—
Let me stop instead and pray.

Please, let me see the way clear,
I'm trapped in confusion and fear.
I can't seem to find what's important to me—
Instead I accept whatever I see.

Please, let me see the way out,
I'm trapped in isolation and doubt.
Each day I feel weaker from a past filled with lies—
I'm caught in my role and still the time flies.

Please, let me see the way home,
I'm trapped and I feel so alone.
I can't make the connections to set myself free—
My life's in a tangle that I try to call me.

Please, let me see the way back
To myself, free at last from this trap.

Fear has become a part of me.
It only takes a look or word
From someone who
Has judged or shouted,
And I am threatened to the core.

I hate fear's familiarity.
It grips me when I hear the yell
Of someone angry.
Adrenaline rushes,
Again I'm victim of my plight.

Fear is always in my company.
I think it's gone, then I'm undone
By someone cruel
Who violates
Bullying, controlling everything.

Free me of this anxiety.
Replace this fear with faith
That I am someone
With value and strength.
I will not be afraid.

I pray I can see the way clear
Through the shadows of terror and fear
And find Your pure light
To guide me this night
Away from the trap I'm in here.

I pray I can choose the right course
To direct me away from remorse
Forgetting my guilt
Believing I've built
A pathway to love at its source.

I pray I can journey through pain
Trusting I'll find joy again
Circling home
Returning alone
Without fear, without hate, without blame.

Please help me over these worries,
The stomach knots won't go away.
I know I shouldn't be frightened,
But I can't see a path through today.

Please help me over these willies,
The *what-if*s my mind cannot see.
I know I can meet today's problems.
I can handle what happens to me.

When dark is closing in on me
And shadows seem to meet,
When I worry about things I shouldn't
And I cannot seem to sleep,
When I make a place for dreams to come
But fear can only creep—
Then let me trust in God's great love
So I don't have to weep.

When I'm lying so still I dare not breathe
And waiting for the light,
Anticipating awful days,
Immobilized with fright,
When I would give just anything
To flee from this black plight—
Then let me sleep, for I am safe,
God watches me tonight.

Take Joy
in the
Moment

May I take this moment
To listen to my self
Turn off mind's chatter
Silence the voices
That interrupt prayers
And hear the rush
Of spirit's release.
May the soft sweet murmur
Of childhood's singing
Reach down deep
Into regions unknown
And find Love waiting
To show me the way.

Let me be just for this moment,
Find ways to like what I'm doing here.
For every hour that's lost to worry
Could be lived in joy, not fear.

Let me be just for this moment,
What is past cannot return.
There isn't time to spend regretting
Things I've never done or learned.

Let me be just for this moment,
Love me for the girl I am.
Life is nothing but this moment
Feeling joy in God's great plan.

How will I embarrass myself today?
I ask, head down, not looking around,
What tortuous price will I have to pay
To hide my shame, but there's one to blame.
I know why I dread each day at this school
I'm no one at all, as I walk down the hall.
I'm such a dumb jerk, I'll never be cool.
Cardinal rule number one, never trust anyone.

Will I get a chance when I leave this place?
Start now to be what is locked inside me.
Can I take a risk and not feel the disgrace?
I know I am strong. Taking risks is seldom wrong.
Let me live a life based on love, not on fear.
I need to be hounded, completely surrounded.
With belief in myself, the answer is clear.
I know I am right. I can win this fight.

Each moment of the day
Can be a miracle
For beauty shines
If I look with truthful eyes
And love grows
If I give with a generous soul.

Each minute of the day
Can be a miracle
For wisdom builds
If I learn with an open mind
And joy comes
If I live with love in my heart.

As I open the door may I notice
Nature's rebirth all around—
Pale green shoots on the dogwood in front
Gay daffodils covering the ground.

In the spring of my life may I follow
Nature's blueprint as my guide
And find in each creamy white crocus
Proof that my soul is alive.

If I look as closely as I possibly can
At a leaf or a petal or seed
If I stop what I'm doing to carefully observe
A grass blade, clover, or reed,

Then I see in the pattern, the color, the line
Of each stem or each root or each pod
How creation is part of my life here on earth
In each perfect fingerprint of God.

Oh my! I think I felt it.
The soft caress of an angel.
I was open
I was patient
On my shoulder
The gentlest touch.

Oh my! I think I heard it.
The glorious singing of an angel.
I was loving
I was truthful
I listened to
Those joyful notes.

Oh my! I think I saw it.
The golden light of an angel.
I was giving
I was helping
I looked around
And there she was.

Let me take from this moment
Just one memory I can treasure
When everything came together
In the brilliance of the day.

Let me capture sweet emotions
How I felt and how I acted
So when all else is subtracted
I'll recall I felt that way.

Let me hold my breath in waiting
Inhale deeply all the magic
Use it when there's something tragic
When I'm lost or gone astray.

Let me never forget the feeling
A secret joy, a special token
My memory's link will not be broken
When I visit it to pray.

When I can't find a way to express my pain
When I'm tied up in knots with fear
When there's not enough time
To do all the tasks
To be all the people I think I must be
Then I turn to myself and I pray:
"Stop trying to square the circle of life.
Instead find the center and stay."

May I daydream through the hours
Take time to whirl among the flowers
Lifted up on prancing horses
Strengthening my self's resources.

Let my voices all be silent
For a moment self-reliant.
No one judging or accusing
To make me nicer or amusing.

Like a bird, I'll fly through sunsets
Touch the waves and tangle fishnets
Soaring high above my troubles
Light and free as breeze-blown bubbles.

Let me grow toward the light
Like a plant, always trusting
It's part of nature's plan
To live each day reaching higher.

Let me grow toward the light,
Girl to woman, always changing
Gather strength with my decision
To live each day feeling love.

Let me grow toward the light,
Cell by cell, always building
Adding energy and power
To live each day giving back.

Being Honest About Myself

May I find a way to touch
Emotions that I fear so much,
Feel them, face them as they are
Instead of running fast and far,
Knowing I'll survive the pain
When I break the heavy chain
Of pretense crafted link by link
So I would never have to think
About those feelings deep inside,
About the times I've lied and lied
To keep the disappointment still,
To silence screams of anger shrill.
May I find through honesty
Belief in God that works for me
Before my heart is broken wide
And I can't find myself inside.

Help me find the place inside
Where I can wait for strength to come
To tell the world that I have lied
About myself and all I've done.

Help me find the trust to tell
The self I used to know by name
How all the truths that I lived well
Are hidden under lies profane.

Help me find the faith that God
Whose trust I have again betrayed
Will love me though I've been a fraud
So I'll forgive the lies I've made.

Please forgive me for hurting
This self that I love
Because I'm insecure inside.
I know that I've misled and lied
And then I'm even more confused
Because of other lies I've used
Until my self becomes so lost
For all the times I've double-crossed
That there is nothing I can do
But come, head bowed, in prayer to You.

To everyone else I'm creative and bold
To everyone else I'm quite fine
To the outside world success is my game
To the outside world luck is mine.

But they don't understand what is happening inside
They don't detect the confusion
They don't know what I go through at night
The struggle I have with illusion.

I wish I could say what I go through
I wish I could show my true soul
I want to be real, not perfect.
Perfection takes too great a toll.

My body's poised for flight—
Ready to run
If I'm found out,
Ready to make tracks
If my mask is pulled off
With its plastic smile
Pretending to please
While underneath black anger howls.

My body's poised for flight—
Ready to disappear
If I'm uncovered,
Ready to lose itself in the crowd
If I'm unraveled
Because one lie isn't woven tight
And a ragged hole appears
Revealing the masquerade inside.

My body's poised for flight—
Ready to leave the scene
If I'm confronted,
Ready with apologies and defenses
If I'm stripped bare
Of pretense, forced by the world
To show my true self
The loving face of God.

Can You help me to be honest?
Reality builds strength in me.
I don't need to make up stories
Or wear a mask so they won't see.

Can You help me to be open?
I know what is right and wrong.
Every lie will make me weaker
Every truth will make me strong.

Sometimes I so hate myself
I feel such pain inside
I'm afraid I'll be caught
Being someone I'm not,
I'm afraid they'll know I have lied.

Sometimes I so fear the day
I can't get myself out of bed,
I'm quite sure I'll be hurt
I'll be treated like dirt
For a moment I'll wish I were dead.

Sometimes I so ache for love
And the need for support from a friend
That I'll reach out to heal,
With truth I'll reveal
Myself, and my pain starts to end.

Each day I'm masked to meet the world—
A mask pretending honesty,
A downturned look, politely sad, when underneath
    I'm really glad,
An angry scowl, saying life's unfair, when actually I
    couldn't care.
Sincere is good, the eye-to-eye, when trying to hide a
    total lie.
A knowing smile is useful, too, when I don't have the
    slightest clue.

My favorite is the stone-face blank—
The mask protecting what I feel.
This mask is dangerous, for it can cling until I'm
    numb to everything.
This mask says my compassion's gone, when in my
    core I know I'm wrong.
This mask protects me from my pain when I don't
    want to hurt again.
Please, Lord, unmask me in Your eyes. I cannot bear
    masks made of lies.

Please forgive me,
I've done something
I'm ashamed of.
I'd like to hide
This lie
In a dark place
Where no one can find it
Except You.

MAKING
HARD
DECISIONS

Let me find a way out of self-pity,
These feelings are useless and small.
If I cry over things that I *don't* have
I'll never have much life at all.

Being sorry for myself isn't pretty
When in truth I have more than enough.
The sound of my whining for extras
Should become an alarm to get tough.

I accept life's not fair; life is tricky
And repeating "poor me" just won't do.
I refuse to be victimized further.
I will use all I am and break through.

$\mathcal{I}$ pray that I can recognize
All the guilt, all the shame,
All the anger and the blame
That's been inside me for so long,
That's kept me from becoming strong.

I pray that I can stop denying
These ways of thinking, ways of feeling,
Ways of hurting, and start healing
By throwing all these thoughts away
To clean my house so love will stay.

If heaven's in my heart
And earth's beneath my feet,
Then what I am is in between
As mind and spirit meet.

I pray that I can visualize
What my life offers me,
For I'm the artist of my fate
If love is what I see.

When I'm confused it's difficult
To believe how strong I am,
To release the self inside me
And follow Your great plan.

I don't want to grow up
If growing up means
Fighting and sadness
And loud angry scenes.

I don't want to grow up
If then I must be
Regretful and jealous
With no time for me.

I pray I'll be wise
And truthful and strong
So when I get older
I'll know where to belong.

And the people I choose
Will be people who know
About living God's way
Giving love as they go.

When I whine with self-pity, may I hear it.
When I act self-absorbed, may I see.
When I choose to be selfish, may I listen
When Your voice points it out inside me.

When I speak words that hurt, may I feel them.
When I don't tell the truth, may I know.
When I hide behind silence, may I notice
When You find all the strength I don't show.

When I take without thanks, may I grasp it.
When I can but won't help, may I care.
When I dwell in my fears, may I leave them
When Your Love gives me faith You are there.

Be with me
When I stand
And take their anger
Wordless.
I do not cry
But take responsibility
For myself.

Be with me
When I stand
And hear their judgment
Expressionless.
I do not speak
But take responsibility
For myself.

Be with me.

The war that I fight is internal
My emotions conflict and collide
My battlefield is growing up
My feelings ebb and flow like the tide.

Sometimes it's voices that argue
Until my poor stomach's in knots.
Sometimes it's shudders of fear
Fighting with the faith that I've got.

Sometimes it's *shoulds* versus *want-tos*
That stop me dead in my tracks
As they battle over my choosing
The right or the wrong way to act.

I know this war will continue
For growing up never will end.
So all I can do is fight bravely
With Love as my general, my friend.

May I have self-discipline
To do the work I must
In order to continue
To grow a self I trust.

May I keep my body healthy
And educate my mind
Give of myself to others
Leave childish wants behind.

May I look for opportunities
To choose right over wrong.
May I believe that deep inside
I'm also brave and strong.

Patience.
To work things out
Step by step
Although I doubt
That I will *ever* get it right
Without frustration and a fight
And a screaming fit or two
I'll pass the time 'til I am through.

Reason.
To counter feelings
That mix me up
And leave me reeling,
For if I take the time to think
Instead of rushing to the brink
Of deep despair, then I will win
And spring the trap I'm often in.

$\mathcal{M}$ay I find the
grace to love generously
hope to live joyously
faith to trust effortlessly
courage to risk confidently
strength to wait patiently
charity to give endlessly
compassion to care instantly
spirit to grow eternally.

BOYS

Today I saw him look at her
Although he was with me
And nothing he could do or say
Would soothe my misery.

For even though I joke and laugh
Pretending we are fine
A knowing voice inside me says
That he's no longer mine.

Please help me find the strength
To trust that what will come
Is for the best. It's over now.
We had our love. It's done.

And when I'm all alone again
Closed down by all my fears
May You be there to comfort me.
Your Love will dry my tears.

I pray for a boy to share with me
A boy who'll just be there for me
To kiss my lips
And stroke my cheek
Who'll hold me tight
When I feel weak
He'll tell me it's okay.

I pray this boy is right for me
That he will be a light to me
He takes my hand
And wipes my tears
And stands with me
Against my fears
To make them go away.

I trust that his belief in me
Will multiply the strength in me
And side by side
Respect will grow
As we grow too
For we will know
That love is here to stay.

I am beautiful. Look at me.
I am intelligent. Listen carefully.
I am faithful. Tell me all.
I am steadfast. Dare to fall.
I am giving. Ask away.
I am loving. Dare to stay.
I am funny. Share my smile.
I am patient. Stay awhile.
I am courageous. Trust my heart.
I am gentle. Come apart.
I am playful. Try my game.
I am waiting. Call my name.

Please, let him stop and look my way,
For I have respect for myself today.
I'm ready to help him, to open my heart.
I know all my lines if he'll play his part.
I'm ready to trust, to be honest and clear.
I'll reveal myself without any fear.

Please, let him know what a friend I could be,
If only he'd take the time to see me.
I'm ready to listen, to give him a hand.
I want him to hear that I understand.
I'm ready to smile, to laugh, and to care.
I'm ready to see if there's love we might share.

Give me the insight
To discover his ways.
Give me compassion
To relieve his bad days.
Let me keep my good humor
When he's in a bad mood
Yet demand his respect
If he starts to get rude.

Help me teach him to trust.
Help me teach him to care.
May I be in his corner,
Even if *he's* not there.
Let me lead him with courage,
May I show him God's way
To love and to honor
Each other, each day.

Why can't I give the love that he needs
To my boyfriend?
Why can't I share the life that I lead
With my boyfriend?
What holds me back from showing concern
For my boyfriend?
If I can't relive those first loving days
With my boyfriend,
Then let me find friendship in new caring ways
With my boyfriend.

Make his thoughts known to me
So I'll understand
What he really is saying
When he takes my hand.

Make our feelings familiar,
Responsive and close,
So I'm very clear
About what he wants most.

Make his motives revealing
So I'll be aware
Of how much he respects me
Of how long he'll be there.

Make our conversations
Transparent as glass
So when one needs the other
We don't have to ask.

Make his actions speak volumes
In ways I can read
So I'll know when to follow
And know when to lead.

Make our belief in each other
As strong as can be
So as we grow older
We grow equally.

May belief in myself make him notice.
May my courage focus his glance.
May my humor bring on his smile,
And by smiling, may he give me a chance.

May my intellect draw his attention.
May my beauty force him to see.
May my friendship demand that he open
To the feelings inside of me.

Help me to have confidence
When he asks me to be something I'm not.
I don't want to fight
Or say he's not right,
But my self is the best thing I've got.

Help me to be wise and brave
When he asks me to change who I am
For what he doesn't get
Is that he must respect
My right to be all that I can.

I lie in my bed
Unable to sleep,
Missing this boy
So much I could weep,
Wanting him back
Though others still care,
For only You know
The love that we share.

I lie in my bed
In tears through the night,
Wishing he'd come
And bring back my light.
May I take all these feelings
And pray they will go
To tell him I miss him
And I love him so.

I Am Love—
I Am Me

No matter how painful this time is
No matter how frightened I feel
Let me find time to speak with you
Let me listen and Your words will heal.

No matter how my friends have hurt me
No matter where courage has gone
Let me pray that You will be with me
Let me open my heart to Your song.

No matter how often I'm hopeless
No matter how angry I feel
Let me start each day over in loving
Let me find in my soul what is real.

May I be
Patient with my weaknesses
Proud of my strengths
Respectful of my feelings
Trustful of my instincts
Loyal to my beliefs
Gentle with my pain
Encouraging to my hopes
Soothing to my anger
Sensitive to my needs
Loving to my soul.

May I awake
With heartfelt joy,
Greeting the day
With a song of my self,
Filled with confidence
That I can be
One with my world.
My body and mind are
Connected to Spirit.
My senses awake
To nature's beauty.
A single flower
Or a whole garden
Of colors and smells,
The sounds of a city,
The rush of an ocean
Are mine—
If I greet each day with love.

May every act I take be done with love
May every choice I make have come from love
May every thought I speak be said with love
May every word I read be read with love
May every gift I bring be filled with love
May every song I sing be trilled with love
May every smile I give be laced with love
May every day I live be graced with love.

I hold a secret in my heart
And the secret is love.
I hear a whisper in my ear
And the whisper is love.
I see a dream inside my mind
And the dream is love.
I take the gift life offers
And the gift is love.
I feel the warmth around me
And the warmth is love.

Let me find a way to live
That makes it easy to forgive
The insults, fights, and little jabs,
Sarcastic words that make me sad.
I give them, take them, turn them round.
They cripple me and bring me down.
I don't believe these things I say
To those I love throughout the day.
Often they say the same to me,
So it is hard to set us free
From self-made traps of words that hate.
Please, I hope it's not too late
For me to help us all move on,
Use words for right instead of wrong.

The more I love, the more I care.
The more I see, the more I hear
Of what life really is to me
Not what I think my life should be.

Then I will grow strong from within
To make my choices based on truth
So that each day is mine to own
And I will never be alone.

God, grant me the vision to see
the beauty of Your world
Grant me the voice to speak
the words of Your prayers
Grant me the strength to help
the children of Your creation
Grant me the grace to feel
the joy of Your presence
Grant me the insight to know
the peace of Your Love.

May I give myself credit for the good things I have
    done.
May I give myself love for the joy I've bestowed.

What I accomplished, no one else could do.
What I created, no one else could make.

The love given me, no one else could earn.
The hope deep inside me, no one else could know.

May I take joy in my springtime.
May I have hope in new flowers.
May I feel the warm morning sun
And dance in the rain's gentle showers.

May I take joy in my springtime.
May I sing to the blue sky above.
May I plow my earth for a garden of faith
And grow to live in God's Love.

WHEN I'VE
LOST
SOMEONE

Where does the soul go
When it's released?
Does it turn to the west
Or proceed to the east?
Does it instantly travel
To places unknown
Or linger reluctant
To leave its last home?

For she was there to comfort me,
She told me, "It's okay."
    She stroked my hair
    She kissed my cheek
    She held me tight when I felt weak
    She made hurt go away.

For she was there to comfort me,
She helped me carry on.
    She'd take my hand
    She'd wipe my tears
    She'd stand on guard against my fears
    She'd stay when all had gone.

Still I believe she's there for me,
I sense her in this night.
    She hears my cry
    She soothes my pain
    With faith that one day, once again
    I'll greet with joy the light.

And then, at last, she'll come to me,
Her very soul I'll touch.
        And she will smile
        As she did when
        We were as one, for now, as then
        My mother loves me much.

If I have to say good-bye,
Please let me do it with grace
With love and concern for his passing
With a smile, not with tears on my face.

If I have to say good-bye,
May I think of my family also
And help heal their pain and their anguish
For their hearts hurt as mine, that I know.

May I remember what he told me
May I take his words to heart
To fight for what is true and good.
He always took my part.

He said to trust my instincts
Also to use my head.
His memory still soothes my tears
Before I go to bed.

May I use the strength he gave me
To grow straight, tall, and proud
Of what I am that made us both
Stand separate from the crowd.

For though he's gone, I love him still
For being funny, cool, and smart.
He made me laugh, he brought me joy,
He'll live inside my heart.

Dear Lord, look after my dog,
It's hard for me to let go.
If You could occasionally scratch her ears,
Then she'll be happy, I know.

Dear Lord, she likes a warm place.
I let her sleep on my bed.
If there's a field where she can run,
She'll come home when she wants to be fed.

Dear Lord, could you find her a bone?
I used to sneak her my meals.
If You would love her as much as I did,
Then I won't worry about how she feels.

I ache to be held
And told it's okay.
I yearn to be hugged
'Til the hurt goes away.

Yet I know that I've grown
Too old to be soothed
By a kiss or a touch
When my heart has been bruised.

And only through God
Will I now find what's gone.
The love I have lost,
Urging me on.

May I open my heart endlessly,
For how else will it contain
The anguish felt in every breath,
The deep ache of my pain?

There are no words that I can speak,
No gesture could reveal
The resonance of loss inside,
The agony I feel.

May I open my heart endlessly
Now that my mind is closed—
It can't construct a single thought,
Despair is all it knows.

Now each day begins at dusk,
Each hour brings darker night
Through which I stumble blind with grief,
For I have lost my light.

May I open my heart endlessly
As I did once before,
When he loved me and I felt that love
Would fill me up and more.

He was my life, my everything.
My soul has come and gone.
What's left is dark and empty,
A shadow to carry on.

May I open my heart endlessly,
Believing that I'll find
A glimpse of equanimity
To soothe my tortured mind,

A glimmer of awareness
From faith in Your great Love,
That You alone will keep me going
Until we meet above.

My friends say this day is a wonderful time,
So why do I feel such pain?
They say that this day should be filled with shared joy
And I should try not to cry once again.

They say happy songs are what we should sing,
So why do the notes sound off-key?
They say that compassion is what it's about,
But there's no caring left inside me.

They say being together is the greatest of fun,
So why do I want them to leave?
They say that tradition supports us in life
And lost love is no reason to grieve.

They say to relax and to be here with them,
So why do I want this to end?
I know they mean well, but what I'd like them
    to hear
Is right now, only God is my friend.

Let me put my whole weight down.
I must have faith in You.
My inner strength is gone from me,
Those burdens carried so effortlessly
Now break my heart in two.

Let me put my whole weight down.
No longer brave am I.
I cannot smile through all my tears
Or even soothe another's fears.
All I can do is cry.

Let me put my whole weight down.
For how else can I bear
The loss that's bleeding out my life
So every breath hurts like a knife.
My grief spreads everywhere.

Let me put my whole weight down
Believing You will stay.
Inadequate, helpless, and weak
I cannot hear or see or speak.
All I can do is pray.

GIVING BACK
TO MY
COMMUNITY

I pray that I'll find
The love that is mine
Generous, trusting, and pure.
It waits in my soul,
It's what makes me whole,
It's the answer, the key, and the cure.

I hope that someday
I can share in some way
The love grown inside me from birth.
For the love that I grow
Is a gift that I know
I'll give back as I give to this earth.

What have I done for others today?
What comforting words have I shared?
Who have I helped without having been asked?
What act of courage have I dared?

Whose heart's desire did I joyously fill?
What encouraging words did I speak?
What stand did I take in someone's behalf?
What strength did I give to the weak?

What did I leave that bettered my world?
What gift of time did I lend?
Whose lonely hand did I take into mine?
What love did I show to a friend?

May I take the chance
To give something back to this earth
To save just one tree
To help someone break free
From the poverty starting from birth.

May I know the way
To preserve what nature has made
To clear just one stream
To make true one dream
Of someone who's always afraid.

May I find the strength
To fight for what I hold dear
To protect the small
To hold hands with all
Those who reach out in fear.

I pray for the homeless with nowhere to sleep.
I pray for the hungry with nothing to eat.
I pray for the fearful with no place to hide.
I pray for the hopeless who failed when they tried.
I pray for the sick ones who can't seem to mend.
I pray for the lonely who can't find a friend.
I pray for all children, those near and those far.
God bless them and keep them wherever they are.

$\mathcal{I}$ know there's a reason I'm here on this earth.
I believe that we all have a mission.
I hope as I grow I'll discover my plan
When I'm faced with important decisions

Like what should I do and where should I go,
What does life want out of me?
It's hard when I'm young and unable to find
The answer to what I should be.

Perhaps the answer's unclear for a purpose
And *should*s are the wrong way to go.
If I trust in myself and follow what's right
Then my mission I surely will know.

Often I'm so self-absorbed
That I can hardly see
How many people in this world
Have far, far less than me.

It's not that I don't care,
I can't seem to find the time
To think about their suffering
And how I might be kind.

My generous spirit's there,
I know what I must do:
Stop talking and start acting now.
By giving I get You.

Let me pause and look for a way
To give to the poor and the helpless today.
To find time during hours when it's all joy and song
For mending a heart, for righting a wrong.

May I take a few moments of grace
To wipe away tears from someone's sad face.
To make gifts of love for those who are lonely,
Using talents for others, and not myself only.

No matter how self-absorbed I am
In my feelings, my worries, my pain,
When I see someone who needs my help,
Quick! Let me reach out again.

No matter the challenges facing me
As I leave my childhood behind,
When I find someone who's hurting,
Quick! Let me do something kind.

No matter what I decide I must do
To prove I am taking a stand,
When I meet someone who's lonely,
Quick! Let me give her my hand.

I grow richer by giving
To someone with less than me.
I grow stronger by weakening
The barriers I build against their world.
I grow taller by bending
To grasp their hands and pull them up.
I grow deeper by releasing
My love to ease their pain.

I have faith in myself
In the person I am—
I will help others
Whenever I can.

I take pride in myself
In the giving I do—
I don't discount my effort
Though my gift isn't new.

I have trust in myself
In the caring I leave—
For the more that I give,
The more I receive.

GETTING MYSELF
BACK
ON TRACK

Let me lift my soul up high
Turn it to the healing light,
Peel back the withered parts to find
New shoots of faith curled tight.

Let me grow my soul with tears
That fall as I begin to see
Why deepest Love is all I'll know
Of God's Eternal Mystery.

The sadness in me is so heavy
That I stoop against the pain.
It's been months since I looked skyward
For stars to wish on once again.

Do I have reason for the wasting
Of every day in deep despair
When You surround me with Your offers
Of infinitely wondrous fare?

The knot of hurt is quite familiar.
I can't imagine it not here.
I'm bound so tightly to my feelings
I can't free myself from fear.

Yet am I not my own creator?
Can I not find my own light?
May I stop this painful hurting
To love—and win this fight.

The world that I see
Is a reflection of me.
It's not what is real,
It mirrors what I feel.
If I make my own trap
It's hard getting back
To a self that is whole
Where I'll meet my own soul.

If I only can stay
On Your track every day,
Circling back where I came,
Finding love and not blame,
Then one time I will know
When my trap lets me go:
I shall see the grand sight
Of a world bathed in light.

Please give me the strength
To break out of this cell.
This cycle of hating
Has made my life hell.

This eating and purging
And eating again
I'm desperate to change,
But can't seem to begin.

Please help me to fight
This awful obsession.
Each day I eat food
In the deepest depression.

I'm caught in a trap
Of my own subtle making.
Oh God, help me heal,
For my whole self is aching.

$\mathcal{I}$ pray for ways to silence
These voices in my head:

The voice that shouts the orders
From the moment I awake,
Then judges when I falter,
Saying, *"You're good for nothing!
How guilty you should be!"*

The voice that whispers, *"Worry
About things that could go wrong."*
Says, *"Security is fleeting.
And tragedy is near.
How fearful you should be!"*

The voice that screams in frustration,
"No one understands your pain."
Points out how unfair life is
And urges me to give up, saying,
"How angry you should be!"

I know that there are voices
Quite different from these three,
Voices saying, *"Have hope. Give love."*
That come from the soul in me.

Now let these fill the silence.

Why am I so frustrated?
It seems all I do is cry.
I can't seem to find my way here.
Sometimes I just want to die.
I review the weeks behind me,
How I've worked to find new friends . . .
Waiting for invitations . . .
Suspense that never ends.

So let me build *my* place here,
Create my own version of home.
I'm tired of second-guessing.
I'm tired of being alone.
I know inside I'm stronger
Than this person that they see
I'm asking for Your help now.
I will find friends just like me.

There's anger inside me that stays hidden away.
It's an anger handed down from my past to today.
If I'm centered and calm, then it seldom shows up,
But when I get fearful, it often erupts.

Please help me, please help me keep anger at bay.
When I'm feeling upset, please lead anger astray.
Give me the strength to react peacefully.
The more love I give, the less anger hurts me.

May I have the patience
To get back on track
When I don't know the answers
And life seems out of whack.

May I know the solution
For whatever will come
Is being open to life.
What is over is done.

May I just keep silent
When thoughts aren't yet clear,
And listen to You
Speak words I can hear.

May I seek out quiet
Until I can see
That the way to solutions
Comes from inside me.

When I see my body changing
Almost before my eyes,
When I worry about my skin,
My hair, my face, my hips, my thighs,

When I sense my feelings rushing—
New emotions raw and clear—
When in just one hour I swing
From purest bliss to deepest fear,

Let me trust I'm God's material
Through which God's energy goes
And my feelings are expressions
Of what God already knows.

My confusion, my anger, my frustration bursts.
I explode in a scream of despair.
I can't find my way to the garden.
I've strayed and now it's not there.

My fury, my sorrow, my loneliness builds.
I hit back against those who love me.
I can't find a way to apologize
Because I'm shut tight and can't see.

Please show me a way to replace all this pain
With compassion, courage, and peace.
Please give me the strength to reach deep for
    forgiveness,
For inside lies the key to release.

May I always keep
A key to my self
Where I can find it
When my actions, reactions,
Mimic others'
And I search through
Identities
Lost and confused.

May I always keep
A pathway to self
Where I can find it
When my deepest fears
Consume me
And I cry silent tears
Anguished, alone,
A child in pain.

Opportunities
to Be
Grateful

Let me dream horses that run in the waves
Let me dream blue ice in jewel-bedecked caves
Let me dream laughing with friends on the beach
Let me dream winning points that only I reach.

If dreamless sleep leaves me restless and bare
Let me dream cloud-dancing with stars in my hair
Let me wake slowly with joy in my heart
Let joy stay with me and never depart.

May I pray with thanksgiving
Instead of complaining
Or asking for life to improve,
For only by trusting
That God's gifts surround me
Will I find the joy that
None can remove.

May my prayers be blessings
And songs of great praising
Not pleas to escape from my past,
For only by seeking
Your presence inside me
Will I find the Love
That will make my joy last.

I pray I'll learn the patience
To let my life unfold
Like the petals of a rose,
To let each day reveal,
When I draw back the curtain,
The light streaming in.

I pray I'll learn the patience
To stop trying to control,
Tear down my defenses,
Take off my armor
Against an unknown enemy
When the enemy is me.

Help me to see with innocent eyes
The sun through the trees
For despite all my tries
I've walked in a fog until just this moment
When Your lightness of being
Answered my cries.

Help me to listen with reverent ears
To the murmuring brook
For despite all my tears
The joy in my life is the sound of Your voice
When the songs of the water
Drown out all my fears.

The music I play is Your gift to me.
Each note sets my quiet soul free.
Day after day the harmonies clear
Repeat and rephrase their sweet tones in my ear.
With the songs that I learn, I play out my part
To express all the feelings that come from my heart.

Thank You, God, for this country,
For its mountains, rivers, and plains,
For the places it offers
To live out my dreams.

Thank You, God, for this nation,
For its spirit of freedom and faith,
For the beauty it offers
To bring my life joy.

On this the last night of the year
As I celebrate, party, and toast,
Let me think of the twelve months just past
And reflect on what pleased me the most.

Was it the time I was angry,
About to be bitter and curt,
But chose instead to speak from my heart
Words that healed, not hurt?

Was it when I didn't get
The part that I wanted to play
And though the rejection was painful
I held my head high all the day?

Perhaps it was just one brief moment
When self-imposed exile seemed sane
But I risked reaching out to another
And, loving, was loved once again.

Whatever I did I am grateful,
For in all of my actions I grew
And the choices I made that were pleasing
Are the ones to guide me the year through.

Thank You for my mother's love
For her tenderness and caring
For all the ways she lets me know
That her life is for sharing.

Thank You for my mother's faith
For her belief in our connection,
For that treasured link
Is her way of protection.

Thank You for my mother's strength
For her trust in what I do
For her willingness to urge me on
To live each day anew.

I pray that I can always joke
At things I do or say
To keep in true perspective
What really counts each day.

I pray that I can always laugh
Although I may not win
I'll live each moment with the grace
That comes from joy within.

Please give me the wisdom
To learn self-control
So I won't lose my temper
Or make my eyes roll
Over little remarks
That don't matter at all
Or when people desert me
And I take the fall.

Please give me the strength
To keep under wraps
My frustration at others
Who seem to lay traps
To get me in trouble
To make me give in.
Let me rise above them
Keep calm from within.

I BOW
TO MY
INNER SELF

In myself I find the balance
Of body, mind, and soul
That makes each day so joyful
That makes each moment whole.

In myself I find the harmony
Of feeling, want, and need
That makes each hour a gift
That makes each task a seed.

In myself I find perfection
In all I say and do
That makes each gesture loving
That makes each thought from You.

May I be gentle with myself
And give my life this break.
My body needs the time to heal
To take away the ache.

May I be loving of myself
And make each day a gift
By feeling joy in moments found
To give my heart a lift.

May I be patient with myself
And know my choice was right.
My instincts are the ones to trust
To keep me in Your light.

There are times when I go inside myself
To look for people who care.
Through all my mind's files
Their names are in piles
But the people simply aren't there.

There are times when I need solutions
To problems that crop up each day
And I ask myself why
No matter how I try
The problems just won't go away.

These times I must try to be patient
And trust I'll discover the seed
Of the love in my soul
That keeps me quite whole
And brings me whatever I need.

I pray each morning when I wake
Before my mind starts to debate
Just for a moment that I will be
Nothing more or less than me.

I pray this wholeness will become
Easier the more it's done
So as I grow, I'll find more ways
To feel my essence through the days.

I look for the vision
Of what I'm about
Not reeling
But healing
Wounds of my doubt.

I look for explanation
Of my presence on earth
Ask why
Then try
To find reasons for my birth.

I look for my self's center
My soul's inner core.
I question
Seek direction
Accept what life's for.

May I look within and see
My self deep inside of me
Dancing, whirling with delight,
Crystalline energy in light.

May I listen until I hear
My self whispering in my ear
Stories of childhood victories,
My celebration histories.

May I trust enough to go
With my self until we know
How to use the golden key
To unlock the door to me.

My soul is not something I know much about.
It's hard to imagine the sound or the look.
I'm unsure of its color or where it resides.
I wish I could look up its shape in a book.

My soul needs neither water nor air.
It doesn't need exercise, clothing, or food.
Yet the older I get, the stronger it grows
Whenever I make a choice that is good.

My soul seems connected to more than myself.
It gathers these feelings that help me to grow
And offers them up to the spirits beyond
Who watch me far more than I know.

My self does not recognize boundaries.
My self will not stay in the box.
My self is not fond of orderly lines,
Restrictions, prescriptions, constrictions, or fines.
My self cannot *stand* chains or locks.

My self often exhibits bad manners.
My self likes unconventional means.
My self chooses work when it feels like play,
Creating, relating, meditating all day.
My self loves to fly in my dreams.

It's easy to hear all the powerful words
The loud-sounding *nos* held deep inside
The taunts and the teasing from long, long ago
The *not-good-enoughs* and all the *can't-dos*
Each word hidden by feelings of fear.
Let each of these words, once found, disappear.

So now I will seek more powerful words
The joys of a *yes* from earlier times
The praises and smiles and pats on the back
The *try-its* and *good-jobs* and *please do your bests*.
May each of these words, cloaked in delight,
Open door after door to life's welcoming light.

I must have faith that what I'm doing
Has greater purpose than I see
And open up my heart in trust
For all You've planned for me.

I must be still and listen
To what my self tells me to do
And let it guide me on the path
That keeps me straight and true.

I must believe that there's a reason
For each decision that I make
And as I learn to choose what's right
I'll choose Your path to take.

FINDING
GOD

On this shortest day of the year
May I treasure the warmth of God's light
As it shines on the paths I could follow
Gilding each one that is right.

May my faith keep me safe through the evening
When even the candlelight's gone
And my soul reaches out for His ember
To glow in my heart all night long.

Two words sustain me, that is all
Two words to trust in when I call
Two words to whisper when I fall
When I'm so broken I must crawl:
"I Know."

I heard those words a single time
They filled me with God's light divine
My soul reached out to make them mine
For I had cried for just one sign:
"I Know."

What I would give again to hear
Voiced Love so intimate, so clear,
Two words that freed me from all fear
Their essence is what I hold dear:
"I Know."

God can make the snow fall in a winter's night.
God can raise the sun to bring the morning light.
God designed birds' wings so they can fill our sky.
God is present at our birth and also when we die.
God knows what we mean no matter what we say.
God is in me now and will be every day.

God can hear me when I cry myself to sleep.
God can feel my pain when I'm afraid to weep.
God is in the heart of every living thing.
God is every leaf that buds in early spring.
God shows me the path when I have lost my way.
God is in me now and will be every day.

As I sit at this table
Let me take time to think
About how You made
What I eat and I drink.
The best way to be thankful
Is to choose what is best
For my mind and my body
And to leave all the rest.

As I sit at this table
With my family and friends
Let me take time to reflect
How Your Love never ends.
The best way to be grateful
Is to choose from my plate
The food that is healthy
To be strong for Your sake.

Thank you for the towering mountains
High in the distance all covered in snow.
I've climbed them in dreams as a pioneer girl,
Following the steps of the women I know.

Thank you for the sweet-smelling pine trees
Deep in dark canyons where my soul longs to roam.
How often in past lives have I walked these steep
    trails?
When did I call these grand mountains my home?

Life stretches ahead, day after day.
There's a balance to work, to love, and to play.
I don't need to rush, to panic, to cram,
There's plenty of space to grow who I am.

It seems, though, quite often, there's just not
    the time.
It seems my life's squeezed between narrow lines.
I feel like a puppet, being moved much too fast,
All jangled and tangled; my balance can't last.

Then let me return to the peace and the grace
Of natural rhythms and Your gentle pace.
So I can discover the time I thought gone
As always returning, just like the dawn.

May I look at each day
As an offering from God,
Each morning a present
Of moments to come:
Sunlight on water,
A shared smile,
Perfection in a rose.
His touch
Tied with caring and courage,
Criss-crossing the hours,
A gift wrapped in love
If only I will open it.

How do I find You?
By loving when I feel angry
By laughing when I feel sad
By giving when I feel selfish
By helping when I feel tired
By caring when I feel sullen
By risking when I feel afraid
By hoping when I feel despair
By praying when I feel alone.

You live in my heart
You sing in my soul
You smile through my eyes
Your love makes me whole
You color my dreams
You take away strife
You calm my worst fears
Your love gives me life.

I am Your child—I am innocent
I am Your creation—I am beautiful
I am Your gift—I am humble
I am Your hope—I am willing
I am Your wisdom—I am understanding
I am Your laughter—I am joyous
I am Your grace—I am compassionate
I am Your Love—I am me.

PRAYERS
FOR
MY SELF

About the Author

CELIA STRAUS is a writer and speaker on adolescent
self-esteem and spirituality. She is also a
screenwriter, with over 150 top professional awards,
and lives in Washington, D.C., with her husband and
two daughters. The author of the book *Prayers on
My Pillow: Inspiration for Girls on the Threshold of
Change* and the spoken-word CD "I'm More Than
What I Seem," Straus continues to answer requests
for prayer-poems from girls and women of all ages
who visit her Web site at www.girlprayers.com.